IT'S A GOD THING

HEARTWARMING STORIES OF FAITH,
FRIENDSHIP, AND BLESSINGS

RENA YEAGER

ALASKADREAMS
PUBLISHING

It's A God Thing

By Rena Yeager

Published by Alaska Dreams Publishing

1st eBook Edition July 2024
1st Paperback Edition July 2024
Paperback Print ISBN 13: 978-1-956303-22-3
Please visit www.alaskadp.com for links.

DEDICATION

First and foremost, I would like to dedicate this book to my Lord Jesus Christ for giving me the ability to write, the passion for writing, and the stories to write. He gave me the words. I write for His glory!

To all my family on both the Yeager side and the Galloway side, thank you for being an important part of my life.

I am so very fortunate and very blessed to have so many wonderful people in my life, and I thank God for every one of you! This book is dedicated with love to all of you! May God bless all of you the way He has blessed me!

CONTENTS

1
———

THE BLESSING OF FRIENDSHIP

What is friendship?

Friendship is defined as a relationship of mutual affection between people. It is a stronger form of Inter-personal bond than an acquaintance or an association such as a classmate, neighbor, coworker, or colleague.

riendship is one of the greatest blessings God has given us and should be treated with love, care, and respect and should never be taken for granted. I am a firm believer that God brings people into our lives that He knows we will need to get us through the situations of life.

I remember when I was about six years old and

in first grade. I came home crying because I didn't have any friends and was sure that I would never have any. My Mom had a chalkboard on the kitchen wall that she often used to write the grocery list. On this day when I came home in tears and voiced my worries about not having friends, she took a piece of chalk, went over to the chalkboard, and said that every time I came home after school and had met a new friend, we would write that person's name on the board, and before long we would have a long list of names.

A couple of days later, I went with Mom to visit a friend of hers. I opted to sit outside on the porch because at six years old, it seemed more fun than sitting in the house listening to two ladies chatting. While I was sitting on the porch, a girl about my age walked by. I recognized her from school, a new girl who had just joined our class a day or two before. It appeared that she recognized me also, as she waved. I ran over to say hello. After a few minutes of talking, she invited me to her house for an ice cream cone. After gaining permission from my mom, I walked with her two blocks to her house. And there, over vanilla ice cream in a sugar cone, Linda became my first friend and was the first name on Mom's chalkboard.

That was over 55 years ago. After high school, our lives went in different directions, but through it all, our friendship remained.

Just like Mom had said, there was soon a long list of names on that little chalkboard in the kitchen.

During my school years, I made many friends, many of whom I remained friends with well beyond school, and some I reconnected with in later years. School did not come easily for me, and after I graduated the last thing, I wanted to do was go to college. The thought of spending another 2 or more years in school just did not appeal to me. I hadn't yet decided what I wanted to do, so when my Aunt and Uncle invited me to move out to California to stay with them, my parents and I thought it was a good idea. So off I went. I was both excited and nervous. I knew I would love spending time with my Aunt and Uncle and helping to care for their 10-year-old granddaughter who had cerebral palsy.

One of my concerns was church as I grew up attending church. My Aunt and Uncle were catholic, and I wasn't at all familiar with the Catholic church. However, I was willing to attend with them and learn about their church and beliefs. A few days after my arrival, Aunt Barbara introduced me to their neighbors, a nice young couple. He was a Pastor at a Baptist church. He invited me to join their youth group later that week. I accepted, realizing it would be a way for me to meet people my age. The night of the youth group meeting arrived, and two girls from the group stopped by to pick me up and walk with me the two houses down to the meeting so I wouldn't have to walk into a house full of strangers by myself.

That night, the topic of the bible study was friendship. We were split into several smaller groups, with our assignment to find bible verses that were about friendship. I didn't realize there were so many verses in the bible about friendship. It was a fun study, and one I have often thought of over the many years since. I made a lot of new friends that night. During my five months in California, I got together often with my new friends and made a lot of wonderful memories that will remain with me forever.

Once I came back home, I kept in touch with these friends for a while, but eventually, we lost contact.

I located one of my California friends on social

media, and we reconnected. How fun it was to talk about those months I had spent in California, and the fun we had had. God had brought these friends into my life to make my transition to life in California easier, friends that would help me grow in my Christian walk.

In the years that followed until the present, God has brought many, many friends into my life, friends that He knew I needed.

With the help of social media, I have been fortunate enough to reconnect with friends and classmates from the past, as well as children I babysat who are now married with children of their own.

While working on this story, I spent time researching friendships in the Bible. I found that there were no greater friendships than that of Jesus and his disciples.

John 15:12-15 says "My command is this. Love each other as I have loved you. Greater love has no one than this: to lay down one's life for one's friends. You are my friends if you do what I command. I no longer call you servants, because a servant does not know his master's business. Instead, I have called you friends, for everything I learned from my Father I have made known to you."

There is no better friend than Jesus. He is always there for us, in the good times and the bad. He is always there with a listening ear, a shoulder to cry on, to love and support us, to encourage us.

This is the type of friend we should all strive to be. So, I challenge you—What can you do to be a better friend to your friends? How can you show them love? What can you do daily to show love towards others? Make it your goal each day to show kindness to others, both friends and even those you don't know. A kind deed will never go unnoticed. Not only will it make the receiver feel good, but it will also make you feel good as well.

2

THE BLESSING CHALLENGE

*A blessing is a noun with several different meanings—
the acts or words of a person who blesses; a special favor,
mercy or benefit, a favor or gift bestowed by God, therefore bringing happiness."*

a blessing can be many things, large or small. It can be as simple as saying hello or smiling at someone. It may seem like a small thing to you, but it may mean the world to that person.

Some of my biggest blessings come from working with and spending time with friends. The inspiration for this story came from such a person as this conversation one day with my dear friend and co-worker. She shared with me that when one of her sons calls her and shares with her the events of his day or vents about a bad day, she understands that she may just need to listen. This time of venting can be about work, relationships, or life in general. Everyone needs to verbalize their frustrations. Life isn't always easy. Days don't always go as planned, and sometimes all a person needs is someone to listen. It Doesn't mean they have to agree. Just listen.

After the time of venting, there's typically a time of calm or less emotion. This is the time when I ask them to take a moment and try to find one blessing in their day. It's not a time of judging or correcting their feelings—just to reflect and find one blessing. The conversation always ends with "Thanks Mom and I love you." Kim says her challenge is to do the same and be an example.

Wow! What an awesome idea! I knew right away that I needed to include Kim's wisdom in this book. In the weeks since Kim shared with me, I've made it a point to look for a blessing or blessings in each day. Not only have I found blessings of my own every day, but I have also looked for ways I can be a blessing to others. Not just to my friends and family, but also to people I don't know, people I encounter out in the community. It's not always easy to be positive in a negative world. But in our world where there is so much hatred, we must do whatever we can to bring light to others, we need to take a stand for what we believe in. We also need to make an effort to help others.

While listening to my favorite Christian radio station not long ago, they were sharing stories about paying it forward—people who did nice things for someone, then that person turned around and did something nice for someone, and so on. I decided right then that this was something I wanted and needed to do. So, a couple of times a month when I would go through a drive-thru window, I paid for the car behind me. It gives me a good feeling knowing that this small act of kindness is a blessing to someone. We don't know what others are going through in their lives, and this kindness could make a difference to them.

One Sunday after church, I was at the receiving end of this kindness when I went through the drive-thru at Starbucks, and when I got up to the window to pay, the cashier told me that the car in front of me had paid for my order. It made me feel good and made me realize how others felt when I did this for them.

While working on this story, I did some research on blessings, and the first place I looked was the Bible, the best book ever written.

In Matthew 5:1-12 we have the Beatitudes, eight statements of characteristics and blessings. Each of the eight begins with blessed are you, or blessed are those. I encourage you to look these up and read them, as they apply to us all.

God's word is full of blessings. Yes, it was written 2000 years ago, but everything written in this book can be applied to our lives today. In a world that is constantly changing, there is one thing that will always and forever remain the same. God's love is true. It is everlasting. He blesses us every single day. He performs miracles, just like He did 2000 years ago.

Sometimes the blessing is right in front of us, and we don't even see it.

I would like to challenge you, my readers. I call it the Blessing Challenge. Look for the blessings in your life, in everyday events. Look for things you can do to be a blessing to others. I guarantee that this will bring joy to your heart, and to the hearts of those who are at the receiving end of your acts of kindness.

3

PAWPRINTS ON OUR HEARTS

PETS AS BELOVED MEMBERS OF OUR FAMILY

*A*nyone who knows me knows that I am an animal lover. It is often the first thing people learn about me. Dogs have always been a part of my life as members of my family. Even as a child, our dog was treated as family. I grew up learning that pets are to be treated with love and respect, not just possessions.

Have you ever looked into the eyes of the dogs and cats shown in the advertisements for the ASCPA? Animals that have been abused, neglected, or abandoned? The sadness and pain in the eyes of these beautiful animals is heartbreaking. It is so easy to fall in love with a puppy or kitten, but these adorable babies grow up to be adults and deserve the love of their families. Deciding to bring a pet into your home is a lifelong commitment and not one to be taken lightly as dog lifespans can run from 6 to 14 years or more, depending on the breed. Cat lifespans can run from 13-20 years, also depending on the breed. So, if you decide to bring a pet into your family, love them, care for them, and treat them with respect as a valued family member. You will be rewarded 100 times over by the love and loyalty of your fur baby family members.

But there are times when things happen, and circumstances force you to re-home a beloved pet. In cases like this, people need to find their pet a good, loving home; someone who will love and care for them. There are always people who are willing to adopt a dog or cat that needs to be re-homed, people who will love them as you do.

I had Bojee, an almost fifteen-year-old male Yorkipoo; a cross between a Yorkie and a toy or miniature poodle. During my years with Bojee, I fell in love with the Yorkie. My favorite description of this beautiful breed was that they were a little dog with a big attitude. I collected books, figurines, stuffed animals, and anything I could find. I knew someday I would own another Yorkie.

As Bojee got older and his health began to decline, I knew it wouldn't be long before he either passed away on his own or I would need to make the decision to let him go. I wasn't planning to get another dog while I still had Bojee, as he had been an only dog for fifteen years and I didn't know how well he would adjust or accept another dog.

Radar was an unexpected blessing. I was surfing pets on Petfinder and immediately fell in love with this 10-month-old Shih Tzu. He was in a rescue only 70 miles from my home. After some consideration and much prayer, I contacted the rescue, filled out the application, and brought Radar home a few weeks later.

It was only three months after bringing Radar home that I had to make the heartbreaking decision to let Bojee cross the Rainbow Bridge due to his declining health. After Bojee passed away, I still had Radar. At first, I didn't plan to get another dog, but, within a day or two after Bojee passed, I started browsing at Petfinder.com. After a few minutes, I saw the most adorable picture of a two-week-old female Yorkie at the same rescue where I had gotten Radar a few months earlier.

Right then I knew that this little girl was to be mine. Was it a coincidence that she was at the same rescue where I had gotten Radar? No, it was a God thing. He had answered the desires in my heart. Because I had already adopted Radar from them, I didn't have to go through the usual screening again. I made arrangements immediately to pick her up six weeks later.

From the moment I brought eight-week-old Lexi home, she and Radar became inseparable best buddies.

We went to visit my dad and stepmom. They had a Westie Maltese mix named Jake. It was clear from the beginning that Lexi was the alpha in our little pack. Jake was lying in his bed, and Lexi went over to him, Jake got out of his bed and walked away. Then, she went over to Radar's bed. He also got up and walked away. She was the boss for sure.

Jake and Radar were already buddies and played well together. As they started chasing each other through the house, Lexi joined in and grabbed onto Radar's tail, and away they all went. She sure didn't want to be left out. This was the beginning of a beautiful friendship. It was fun to watch them grow up together, and their puppy antics kept me laughing every day. Not only were they each other's best friend, they were mine. They were my kids and my family.

Several years ago, I moved into a new apartment with Radar and Lexi. The manager at the time allowed me to move in with two dogs. I had only been in my new apartment for a few months when the regional manager went through doing inspections and saw I had two dogs. I was given a lease violation and was told that I had one week to re-home Radar. Because Lexi was on my lease as my registered Emotional Support Animal, it was Radar that would need to go. I was in a panic and heartbroken! How could I possibly find him a good, loving home in just a week? I was sure it would take more time!

I had only moved into this apartment a few months earlier, so moving wasn't an option due to the lease. I would have gladly moved if it meant that I could keep Radar. I knew I had to do something fast. Not knowing where else to turn, I thought that the best way to get the word out of my dilemma was to put it on social media. And I prayed! I prayed for guidance that God would lead me to the right person or family.

When sharing my situation with a neighbor, she suggested I *not* put it on social media, as that is where I would find the scammers. She put me in touch with a couple of people she knew who help people find lost animals, and re-home them if circumstances warranted it. Just a couple of days later, I received a call from a family who were very interested in adopting Radar, and we set up a time to meet the next morning. They lived in a town about an hour or so away from where I lived, and they would drive here to meet us. I prayed before this meeting that these people would choose to adopt Radar, but my heart was heavy at the same time. It would be hard to let him go. The minute I met the couple, Tom and Judi, I liked them and knew they were the right family for Radar. He liked them right away too. We visited for a bit, and I asked them if we could keep in touch. They readily agreed. A short time later, Radar was on his way to his new home with his new family, and Lexi and I were on our way home to our apartment without Radar.

After re-homing Radar, Lexi was affected by this

sudden change in our lives. The day he moved to his new home, Lexi lay on the arm of the couch with her back to me. She was feeling sad too and missed her brother. Some people believe that pets don't understand what we say or that they don't have feelings. But I strongly believe that they do as Lexi's reaction to Radar leaving proves that they indeed have feelings and understand what is going on in our lives. It took several months, and eventually, we both settled into a life of just the two of us, but Lexi was never quite the same. His new family has sent many updates and pictures. Knowing he was loved and happy made my heart smile. It wasn't by chance or coincidence that I found this family for Radar. It was prayer! It was a God thing!

(In May of 2024, I received the sad news that Radar had passed away, a month shy of his 14th birthday. I will forever be thankful to Tom and Judi Stecker for taking him and giving him a wonderful home and loving him as I did.)

When I would leave the apartment before re-homing Radar, Lexi had his company to keep her occupied. Eventually, after Radar was gone and Lexi was alone, I started noticing her developing a mild case of separation anxiety. I distracted her before I would leave by filling her bowl with her favorite food, and then I would slip out the door. This seemed to work well at the time, so I kept it up.

In 2017, I registered Lexi to become my emotional support animal. This title would allow me to fly with her at no cost, and she would be allowed into apartments where animals were otherwise not allowed.

When I went to California for Christmas the next year, I took Lexi with me. She was a great little traveler and remained quiet in her carrier during the 3-hour flight. She became fast friends with Curly, my stepmom Rhondda's dog, and she was welcome wherever we went, even shopping. When we would go visit other family members, she would lie quietly in the stroller.

In the early spring of 2020, the country was hit with Covid-19, and it seemed like the whole world was shut down. Restaurants closed, and only drive-throughs were open. Large gatherings were canceled and discouraged, and masks were mandatory in all public places. That summer many places were on total lockdown. My job, working with people with disabilities meant I was considered *essential personnel,*

so I still went to work. Some days, Lexi would go to work with me. On other days she went to Doggie Daycare and occasionally stayed home alone. On her home days, she would eagerly meet me at the door and greet me with lots of puppy dog kisses and cuddle time.

Lexi turned nine years old a few short months later. I had changed jobs but was still working with disabled people, so Lexi was able to go to work with me on weekends, making her time home alone a bit less. It was also this year that I started looking for a new apartment. The place I was living was full of drug users, and people would often steal packages if left outside apartment doors. The buildings were not secure, and I no longer felt safe here when I would come home late at night.

Later 2021 also brought several changes. Some were good, some not so good. In September I moved into a new apartment. Not only was it new to me, but it was a brand-new building that had opened on September 1st. It was beautiful and I loved it. Covid was still present, but people were finally starting to branch out. With much thought and prayer, I decided to go to California for Christmas that year even though travel was still discouraged. I planned on taking Lexi with me again. We all had to find what our new normal was after Covid entered our lives.

It was on this trip that I started noticing changes in my girl's behavior. She had turned 11 years old in May and was now considered a senior. She did very well traveling, as she had three years earlier, so that was not an issue. Shortly before our arrival, Rhondda, my stepmother who I stayed with while in California, had an accident, so she was in a rehab center for the first few days of our stay. The day after we arrived, we were picked up by my step-brother Dale, his wife Lisa, and Curly to take us to the rehab center to spend the day with Rhondda. In the car, Lexi attacked poor Curly. Not once, but twice. She would go after him several more times that day while we were at the rehab center. In the past, Lexi had always gotten along well with other dogs, and during previous visits, she and Curly had been great friends. I was puzzled by this unusual behavior. I had no choice but to keep her on a leash, even in the house. Although it bothered me to keep her confined, it helped as long as I was at the other end of the leash. If I let her off the leash, she would attack Curly again. He was a gentle dog and never fought back. When we would leave the house and leave both dogs home, Lexi would need to go in the crate, as we were afraid to leave her alone with Curly. We didn't want either dog to get hurt.

Due to Lexi's increased whining and barking, we couldn't take her shopping or visit people's homes. She would need to stay in the car, and I would return to the car several times to take her outside to do her duty. This broke my heart. Each time I had to put her back in the car, she would whine and cling to me. I had never had to do anything like this before, and I couldn't understand why I needed to do this now. Why was Lexi behaving this way? That night I vowed I would never do this to my baby again when we returned to Minnesota.

We went home two weeks later and settled back into our daily routine. As before, sometimes I took her to work with me, some days I left her home and some days she went to doggie daycare. This seemed to work for a few months, but in April 2022 things began to change again. I left her alone on a Friday afternoon as I planned on going shopping after work. She had only been alone for three hours when I got a call from my apartment manager saying that she had received numerous calls from my neighbors stating that Lexi had been whining, crying, and barking at the door all afternoon, and I needed to go home and get her. She had never done this before, and I was concerned that maybe she was in pain, or something was wrong with her, something other than a case of separation anxiety. I took her to the vet the following week. Nothing physical was wrong with her, but the vet gave me some information on something called Cognitive Dysfunction Syndrome, which is similar to that of Alzheimer's in people. CDS often happens to animals any time after the age of nine years, and Lexi was eleven. At that time, the only symptom she exhibited was the increased separation anxiety. But now I knew what to watch for. I researched these symptoms on my own to learn more about this disease, and with a heavy heart, I realized that Lexi and I might be headed down a road unknown to us. From the day I brought her home, she was always there for me and helped me through moments of depression and anxiety. Now it was my turn to pay back Lexi.

The separation anxiety was the first big change I noticed. I could live with this. I just needed to always plan ahead. I could no longer leave her home alone, so during the week she would either go to work with me or go to daycare at Bubbles and Bows. On my work weekend, she would go to work with me, but on my weekends off I would stay home because I didn't feel that I could leave her, not even for a little while. I couldn't go to church or make plans to go anywhere. But I accepted this, as I would do whatever I needed to do to keep her healthy and happy. On the rare occasion when I would have to leave for an hour or two, my good friend Gina would come to my rescue and keep Lexi. It was a great discovery when, a couple of months later I found out that our daycare was open on weekends. I was able to start going to church again and make plans with friends.

The hardest part of caring for a dog with dementia, just like with people, is the behavior changes. In a matter of months, her behavior again changed. She had always been a happy little girl who loved everyone and enjoyed going to daycare and for rides in her stroller, she loved playing with other dogs, both big and small. But now, she had become fearful and aggressive, no longer enjoying places she had always loved. I would take her to daycare, and she would attempt to bite me. She would whine and shake. Before this, she had always loved going to work with me, but now I could no longer trust her as I was afraid she would bite the clients. At home, she was calm and quiet with just the two of us. As time went on, it became very clear to me that my time with her was limited. It broke my heart to watch her decline so rapidly. It was obvious that she was no longer enjoying life, and her aggressions were getting worse every day. I knew in my heart that it wouldn't be long before I would need to make the heartbreaking decision to let my baby cross the Rainbow Bridge, to let her run free—free from pain, anxiety, and a life she no longer enjoyed. It would be my final act of love for her.

During the last year of her life, Lexi had become very protective of me. She would aggressively bark at anyone who came close to me. In her eyes, I was her world, and no one better come close to it. On January 3, 2023, I made the appointment with the vet for January 19th, allowing myself two weeks to say goodbye and change my mind if I chose to do so. But every day during those last two weeks, God showed me things that confirmed I had made the right decision.

The day I had dreaded finally came. I can't even put into words the anguish I was going through. I knew it was the right decision, but the pain was almost unbearable. Gina came with me so I wouldn't need to be alone. I held my girl in my arms while waiting for the technician to come in. A short time later, the tech came in to give Lexi a sedative to make her sleep for the rest of the procedure. She left instructions that once Lexi fell asleep, to hit the button on the pager, and she would come back to get her to take her to put the catheter in.

I held her and talked softly to her while she drifted off to sleep. I pushed the button on the pager, and within only a few seconds the tech came back in to get her. As the technician approached me and reached out for me to place Lexi in her arms, Lexi's head shot up and she began barking aggressively at the poor girl, who jumped back. This startled all of us, and we laughed. I'm sure that girl had never witnessed this before, and probably never would again. Lexi defended me to the very end. I know God used this incident to ease the pain that I was feeling. Now when I share with others about this painful day, I smile when I think about how protective of me she was on our last day together. When I chose her name, I had never looked it up to see what it meant, I just liked the name. It wasn't until after she had passed that I researched the meaning. The name Lexi means "Defender of Man." She had certainly lived up to her name, becoming "Defender of Mom." I miss my little girl every day. There's not a day that goes by that I don't think of her. But knowing that she was free has helped heal my heart.

No dog would ever replace her, but another dog would fill the void that Lexi left behind in my heart and life. I would trust God to guide me to the right dog, whether it be a new puppy or an older rescue dog. My faith and trust are in my Lord. He cares about every aspect of our lives.

Psalm 37:4 says, "Delight yourself in the Lord, and He will give you the desires of your heart."

And I know that beyond the shadow of a doubt, He would do exactly that. Even so, life without Lexi was hard making the silence of my empty apartment almost unbearable at times. I missed everything about her, especially our early morning snuggles. As I started thinking about bringing another dog into my life, I knew I needed to be somewhat selective. Living in an apartment, I needed a small dog that was not an excessive barker.

I started researching different breeds. I read books and magazine articles, watched videos on YouTube, and browsed the internet. I was considering the King Charles Cavalier Spaniel, the Shih Tzu, and the Havanese. Each of these breeds fit my criteria, but I finally settled on the Shih Tzu or a Shih Tzu mix, feeling that this breed was perfect for my needs. I joined several Shih Tzu groups on Facebook, read classified ads in the paper, and shared with others what I was looking for, including my good friend Kari. I checked out breeders and rescues and trusted that God would guide me to the dog that He wanted me to have. I knew the right one was out there, and I wasn't in a rush.

Kari and I started texting back and forth about my search for a puppy, or a rescue dog. As it turned out, she was considering getting a mail-order bride for her two-year-old Shih Tzu, Sammy, with plans to breed the two when the new puppy was old enough.

We found that we needed to be very careful during our search because of all the scams out there. One situation involved a breeder who said he lived about 50 miles from where Kari lived. Kari looked up the address on Google Maps and it turned out he lived in Canada. Then we thought we found the perfect litter in Wisconsin. They wanted a large deposit. But something didn't feel right, so Kari contacted the police department in the town and even though they could not confirm that he lived at the address that he had given Kari, the police warned Kari not to send money to that address. We were disappointed again because of the scammers.

I texted Kari about how expensive all the puppies we found were. We couldn't afford to spend $1200-$1400 per puppy. As we talked, we decided there were certain things we wanted in each of our puppies, and Kari said, "Wouldn't it be neat if we could raise sisters?"

"That'd be cool," I answered. I had decided I wanted a female from a young litter that wouldn't be ready for at least several weeks, as I wasn't emotionally ready to bring another dog home.

Kari's criteria were a Shih Tzu or Shih Tzu mix, female, white, and a reasonable price, and our chosen breed, the Shih Tzu, wasn't known as excessive barkers. We both wanted puppies close to where we live. Kari was sitting one day praying about what her puppy's name would be, and Lily of the Valley came to her. When she looked up the meaning of Lily, it meant return to happiness. So, she decided her first name would be Lily. She also gave her a middle name, and it would be Belle. In Hebrew Belle means God's Oath.

I was sitting at work one night when I got a text from Kari. "I may have found a batch of two-week-old puppies that are one-half Shih Tzu. I'm not sure what the other half is yet. She had five puppies this time, surely at least two are female." Kari also shared with me the story of how she found this new litter. She had been over at her sister Jeani's, and she mentioned her boss had to take her friend and very pregnant Shih Tzu to Babbit to her mother's house about 90 minutes from where we live. The breeder, Tina, was asking $400 without first shots, and more if they were to have their first shots. She told me not to get excited. It turned out that two of them were girls, so how could I not get excited? So far, these puppies sounded exactly what we were praying for. It didn't take us long to decide that these girls would be ours. Although we were praying for different things, God answered both of our prayers in a special way.

We received our first pictures of the girls and Kari asked if she could have the little girl with the black nose. I was more than happy to take the little girl with the pinkish nose, as they were both adorable.

Since Kari had named hers, I needed to choose a name for her sister. I looked through books and tried out several different names, but nothing seemed right. I thought back to how it had been by the grace of God that we had found these beautiful girls when it hit me. Maybe I should name her Gracie! I tried this name out several times to see how it would sound, and how it would fit. But before I finalized her name, I looked up the meaning; Gracie means blessed. That's when I knew it was perfect. I've never been one to give my dogs middle names, but Kari had named hers Lilly Belle and we have another friend who has a Maltese named Daisy Mae. So, I decided giving her a middle name might be fun, but what should it be? My first thought was Rose. Gracie Rose sounded nice, but it didn't feel quite right. I kept looking for the perfect middle name and tried out several, but none seemed to fit. Another name on my list was Ruth. Although the name sounded good and I liked it, it wasn't a favorite. I looked up the meaning which turned out to be *a compassionate friend*. Gracie Ruth… *blessed compassionate friend*. Yes! I had found the perfect name for her.

In March 2023 when the puppies were 8 weeks old, we arranged to meet Tina to bring our girls home. Since it was only two weeks until Easter, the puppies were brought to us in cute little Easter baskets. The story doesn't end with our girls as there were five puppies in the litter. Our two girls and three adorable little boys. These boys found homes with two friends of Kari's.

Since then, Kari, I, and our girls get together frequently for playdates at the dog park or each other's houses. It is so fun to watch them get excited when they see each other. Sisters and best friends for life.

Kari and I often marvel at what an answer to prayer we both received when God brought Lilly and Gracie into our lives.

Mark 11:22-24 says, "Have faith in God" Jesus answered. "Truly I tell you, if anyone says to this mountain, 'go, throw yourself into the sea,' and does not doubt in their heart but believes that what they say will happen, it will be done for them. Therefore, I tell you, whatever you ask in prayer, believe that you have received it, and it will be yours."

Our prayers were answered, and each day we give thanks for these two very special blessings.

4

_____

ANYTHING YOU CAN DREAM YOU CAN DO

"If you can dream it, you can do it. Always remember that this whole thing was started with a dream and a mouse." Walt Disney

*A*nything we want in life we need to work for. Nothing comes free. And often, things we want begin with a dream.

As a senior in high school in 1981, I looked forward with great anticipation to finally getting out of school. I didn't know what life had in store for me but like any teenager, I was looking forward to moving forward.

All the seniors were given a questionnaire to fill out. We were told to write down three things that we hoped to accomplish during our lifetime.

After much thought and consideration, I knew what I wanted to write. I had three things, three dreams that I hoped to fulfill someday.

My first dream was to someday find my birth family. I had been adopted at the age of two years old and I wanted to know and learn my history.

The second dream was to someday have a daycare center of my own. I had begun babysitting at the age of 12 and loved children. I knew that I wanted to continue working with children, and having my own daycare center would be perfect.

My third dream was to become a published author. I started to write stories at the age of 14 and had a passion for writing. I was seldom seen without a notebook and a pen in hand.

Graduation came and went, and my 12 years of schooling were over. High school had been difficult, Although I could read and spell, I had trouble with comprehension and often couldn't understand or remember what I had read, which made studying very difficult. Math was the worst. Anything beyond basic math made no sense to me at all. And sometimes, even basic math was beyond my comprehension. I wasn't sure I wanted to continue my education by attending college. I didn't know it at the time, but God was working in my life to prepare me for my future.

As summer came to an end, and fall fast approaching, I needed to decide what I wanted to do. Go to college? Get a job? I had spent the summer babysitting, but I surely couldn't babysit for the rest of my life. And what kind of job could I get without a college education? But still, I wasn't sure college was for me.

At this time, my aunt and uncle who lived in California, invited to me come out there to stay with them for a while.

After discussing this with my parents, we decided that this would be a good experience for me to try new things and think about what I wanted to do with my life.

So, on an evening in October 1981, my plane landed at the Los Angeles airport, and I began my new life in Torrance California.

My Aunt Barbara and Uncle Book were raising their 10-year-old granddaughter Alicia, who had been born with Cerebral Palsy.

During my 5 months living in California, I

learned how to help take care of Alicia, attending several of her school days. I enjoyed going with her to school and enjoyed helping her and just spending time with her.

I had also gotten a job at a nearby daycare center. My time there confirmed that yes, I did want a career working with children.

Before I knew it, it was time to come home to Minnesota. By then, I decided that I would attend our local junior college in the Fall, and major in Human Services.

I spent three years in college and got my degree in Human Services, graduating in 1985.

It had been 4 years since filling out that questionnaire in high school, and I found myself thinking about it. The three things I had listed seemed unreachable, just a few dreams that I didn't think I could reach.

About this time, I began babysitting for a good childhood friend. She and her husband had bought my parents' house, the house I had grown up in. During my years of babysitting for them, we began talking about the possibility of opening a daycare center in their basement. We looked into it to find out what we would need to do and decided to move forward with our plans.

So, in 1992, after licensing and inspections by the fire Marshall were completed, Little Oaks Day Care opened its doors. We chose our name from the phrase, *mighty oaks from little acorns grow.* That, and because the house was located on Oak Street. Having my own daycare was a dream come true. A dream I never really thought would happen. But God put the right people into my life and made it all possible.

I had originally begun to search for my birth family in 1986. At the time of my adoption in the 60s, adoption records were sealed, so gaining information was no easy task. But again, the Lord knew the desires of my heart, and in 1994, with the help of an adoption group in Seattle and the support of my family, my birth family was found, and I flew out to Seattle to meet them.

Two of my dreams had come true. Now I only had one dream left that I had written down on that questionnaire in high school those years ago. I started writing stories at about the age of 14. At that time, I mostly wrote about TV shows, whichever was my favorite at the time. I learned that writing was sort of an escape for me, It helped me get away from the real world. It became a passion. I'm not sure what happened, but in the mid-90s I just suddenly stopped writing.

Then in 2000, I was introduced to the world of fan fiction, where people could write stories about movies, books, or TV shows and post them on the internet fan fiction site. I was hooked, and I began writing again. I still wrote about TV shows, although I wanted to break away from them and start writing my own stories, with my own characters. But I didn't think I was a good enough writer or creative enough to accomplish this. I was enjoying writing fanfiction and thought posting stories on the site would be the closest I would ever get to being a published writer.

During the mid-90s, I had written two stories that were not related to TV, but I pretty much kept them to myself. Until years later when I gave them to a dear friend to read. After she had read them, she suggested I talk to a co-worker of ours who had a publishing business, so, I did. He read the stories and decided he would work with me on developing my writing ability. We spent much time together working on ideas, teaching me different methods of writing, and setting goals. I started a book of short stories, and sixteen months later, it was completed. In October 2020 my first book was published. Thirty-nine years after I had filled out that questionnaire. One year before my 40th high school reunion.

I had pretty much given up my dream of becoming a published author. But am very thankful that I didn't. It took almost forty years for this dream to become a reality. If I had given up, this dream never would have come true.

I continue to write, with the goal of getting more books out. God guided me every step of the way to make these dreams come true. He gave me the gift of writing, and I write for His glory.

5

SPECIAL OLYMPICS, SPECIAL MEMORIES

"Let me win, but if I cannot win, let me be brave in the attempt."

hose are the words to the special Olympic oath written by Special Olympic founder, Eunice Kennedy Shriver in 1968. This oath is recited at the beginning of each Special Olympic event. The words emphasize the importance of effort and trying for one's personal best.

I first became involved in this wonderful program through my job as a direct service professional. I was working in an adult foster home with people with disabilities. Several of my clients were involved in Special O bowling and track and field. I enjoyed taking them to their practices each week but that didn't compare to the feelings I had when I went on my first bus trip with my client to the regional Special O track and field games.

The event began with the parade of athletes as each team was introduced to the spectators in the stands. My client, a man with Down Syndrome, was all smiles as we made our way down the track. After the parade of athletes completed their walk down the track, they stopped in front of the crowd, where we recited the oath, and someone sang the national anthem. Without any prompts whatsoever, my client removed his cap and placed it over his heart. It was such a touching moment and brought tears to my eyes. It still does when I think of it and it will forever be one of my favorite memories of my years involved with Special Olympics.

Several years later, I was asked by my supervisor if I would consider going with this same client to the Special O track and field summer games in Minneapolis. It would be a three-day event, traveling on a chartered bus and staying in a motel. I wasn't so sure about this, as it was way out of my comfort zone. It would mean being with 40 athletes and their families or staff for three days traveling and being with people I didn't know. There was nothing about this that sounded like something I would enjoy. Being around large groups of people that I don't know causes anxiety. I was sure I was making the wrong decision, but I decided to go on this trip. I needed to put my fear and anxiety aside. I knew that my client would enjoy himself and his needs had to come first. However, the closer it got, the more I began second-guessing my decision. I was convinced that going on this trip was a huge mistake. But I knew I couldn't back out now, only a couple of days from departure. I was committed.

Many things needed to be done. Getting my client packed and ready to go, making sure nothing was forgotten, and for myself too. The list for preparing and packing for this adventure was a long one. The morning of departure arrived, and we loaded the bus with the athletes, their staff, coach, and family members. My client and I were sort of on our own. Since this was a new thing to me, I had told our coaches to let me know where and when his events were, and I would have him there.

After the four-hour bus ride with only one stop along the way, we arrived at our destination, the University of Minnesota track. We unloaded the bus, got our event schedules from our coach, and were on our own. Everyone went their separate ways. My client and I started walking around, taking in the sights around us. He was a very social person and loved people, so he was all smiles as we walked around watching the people in their various sports and activities. I was mesmerized and totally in awe of my surroundings. It was like nothing I had ever seen before. It was obvious my client felt the same way.

One of the first places we checked out was called Boogie Town. It was a DJ playing music. Both my client and I enjoy music. I took a chair on the side-lines and allowed him the freedom to join his peers as they danced to The Chicken Dance, Macarena, and Locomotion. Boogie Town quickly became our favorite place. We spent most of our free time there when he wasn't competing.

During our three days at this event, all I could think of was "I know there is a story in here some-where." Watching the athletes compete in their many events was amazing. The joy on their faces when they won melted my heart. The award ceremony that followed the events was very touching. The faces of the athletes brought tears to my eyes. They lived the words of the Special Olympic oath, "Let me win, but if I cannot win, let me be brave in the attempt."

People with disabilities can do anything people

without disabilities can do. They just do it differently. From the time they are very small, they are taught to live in a world where they are often secluded due to their disabilities. They are often treated differently for this very reason. But for these three days, those without disabilities were brought into their world. The field was accessible for wheelchairs, walkers, and other adaptive equipment. Everything revolved around different kinds of disabilities. Although this trip had been way out of my comfort zone when I started, it quickly became a weekend that I would remember and treasure.

It became "My Thing" for one weekend every summer for the next 14 years, a time I looked forward to every year with great anticipation. Over those 14 years, things changed. The client I had taken for the first four years, was no longer able to go due to health issues, so I brought another client. Our locations changed, and our coaches changed. But one thing that has never changed has been the excitement and the thrill of watching the athletes compete, the smile on their faces tells the story of pure joy,

Special Olympics is a wonderful program, and I feel fortunate to have been a part of it for as long as I did. I would have missed a great opportunity if I hadn't put my fear aside and gone on this trip that first year. God knew what was best for me, and I followed his guidance. I will forever be thankful that I did. My years involved in Special O gave me memories that I will treasure forever.

6

SEARCHING FOR MY PAST

*I*t had never been a secret in my family that I had been adopted at the age of two years old. I grew up hearing the chosen baby story, a story I enjoyed but didn't understand until I was about 5 or so.

I was born in Everett Washington, near Seattle. I was adopted by my dad, from Yakima WA, and my Mom, from Bemidji MN. My new family also included two older brothers, Bud and Bill. By the time I was four years old, we had moved into our house in Minnesota, and that's where we remained for the next 50+ years. I started my school career in our hometown of Grand Rapids, a small town in northern Minnesota.

At the time of my adoption, my parents weren't

told much about my history or background. All they knew was that I had been the youngest of 7 children, and had been removed from the home by authorities at the age of 6 months. My full name was on my adoption papers, including a last name.

I was in high school when I became interested in learning more about my birth family. Like most adoptees, I had questions about who I was and where I had come from. I didn't think this was something I could talk to my parents about. I felt that by talking to them about my interest in my birth family, I would hurt them or they would think that I wasn't happy with my adoptive family. Nothing was farther from the truth. I loved my adoptive family. But I didn't know if they would understand.

I began watching movies and reading books, anything I could find about adoption and adoptees searching for their roots. I started writing to different groups that were for people who wanted to search for their birth family, whether it be an adoptee, a birth parent, or a sibling. I began getting a lot of information in the mail, and when my mom saw it come through, she told me that if I wanted to search for my birth family, it was fine with them. They would support me and help me in any way they could. She told me it was perfectly natural for me to want to know about my background. Knowing that my parents were behind me, I continued to gather information about search groups. Also knowing I had their support made it easier to talk to them about information that I was getting.

At the time of my adoption in the 60s, adoption records were sealed. An adoptee or birth parent could not gain any information contained in these records without showing good cause, such as a medical emergency or something similar. Being born in Everett Washington, I found out that my records would be kept in the capitol, Olympia. So I wrote to them explaining who I was and what I was looking for and gave them what little information I had. I really wasn't expecting to hear back from them, so was very surprised several weeks later when I received a large manilla envelope from Olympia. My Mom and I sat down together to read the contents of the envelope.

All identifying information had been blacked out, but on these pages were written information about my first two years of life. Some of it was hard to read because I hadn't gotten a very good start in life. I had been born two months premature, the youngest of seven children. I was only 11 months younger than one of my brothers. I was 6 months old when I was removed from the home by authorities. At this time, I had a severe diaper rash and was malnourished. I was placed in a foster home. At about the age of 18 months, my birth parents rights were terminated and I was eligible for adoption.

Off and on over the years, I had contacted several groups about how to search for my birth family. I found myself thinking more and more about my history, and the desire to know more about my past had become very important. I started seriously searching for my birth family in 1986. I had read my birth name on my amended birth certificate so I had a name to start with. Or so I thought.

I joined a group in Seattle called Washington Adoptee's Right Movement, or WARM. I believed that finding an intermediary to conduct the search was the best way to go. In addition to WARM, I also asked for help from my cousin, who lived in Seattle. The last name on my birth certificate was Meyer, so I asked my cousin to send me a list of all the Meyers listed in the Seattle phone book, Being in the 80s, we didn't have Google to help search. I wrote many letters to those people on the list that my cousin had sent, and I even received many replies, but none of them were related to me.

On a trip to Seattle, we wrote more letters and tried to find more information, but to no avail.

My search was a long one. During my search, I would keep in touch with Valerie, the intermediary assigned to my case. I had learned from reading my history that two of my older siblings, a sister, and a brother, had also been given up for adoption.

In 1994 during one of my conversations with Valerie, I had asked her why she was only searching for the one brother who had given up for adoption when there were five other children in the family. Valerie said she wasn't aware of the other children, but was glad to finally know this information so could try to search from a different angle.

It was just a few weeks later when Valerie called and said she had my birth mother's name, and asked if I wanted to know her name. Yes, I said without hesitation. Carol Galloway. My birth mother's name was Carol Galloway. I finally had a name. It wasn't Meyer after all. Valerie went on to tell me that she had passed away in 1986 at the age of 48 from breast cancer. She went on to tell me that she had located my birthmother's older sister, Shirley, and did I want her to give her my contact information. Again, I said yes without hesitation. After all, I had been waiting for this moment for eight years. Later that evening, I received a phone call from my birth aunt. That same evening I spoke with my oldest brother. My dream of finding my birth family had finally come true. I had found the piece of my puzzle that had been missing.

Before I share the rest of the story, I need to interject here with some details that will be important to the rest of the story.

My dad was from Yakima, Washington, and he still had family in different parts of the state, including a sister and many nieces and nephews. His sister had been diagnosed with Lou Gehrig's disease several years earlier, and in 1994, we knew that the time had come to say goodbye to her. So her daughter, the one who had helped me gather information about my birth family, planned a family reunion at her house in Seattle for a weekend in the summer of 1994. After chatting with my birth aunt, Shirley, she planned a family reunion for that same weekend. Not knowing how long they would need to be there for my Aunt, my parents drove out to Seattle, pulling their camper. I would fly out a couple of weeks later.

When I got to Seattle, my parents picked me up at the airport and drove to my cousin Shelly's house. My dad's younger sister Barbara was also there, along with her daughter. As well as several of the children of dad's other sisters, Donna and Gerry. I hadn't seen any of them for many years, so it was so nice to see them. Shelly would be home from work soon. Once we got to Shelly's, I called my Aunt Shirley to tell her I had arrived, and where I was staying. She said that her brother Roy lived in that area somewhere.

Shelly arrived home a short time later, and I went out to greet her. I told her I had talked to my Aunt Shirley and she had said that her brother Roy lived somewhere in this area. Shelly's eyes got big and she said "Roy Galloway is your uncle? He lives across the street!" Then she asked if I would like to meet him. Of course, I said yes. So across the street we went, and Shelly knocked on the door. When Uncle Roy opened the door, Shelly said "Roy, this is your niece, Rena." The look on his face was priceless, and seemed to say "If she's my niece, what is she doing with you?" Shelly laughed and said, "She's also my cousin." He invited us in and I met his wife, Kay. While we were there, his daughter Kerry called and he told her about me, and that I was sitting in his living room. Even today, many years later, this is the most amazing part of my story and it was definitely a God thing.

The next day, Saturday, was the family reunion of

my Yeager side of the family. It was a bittersweet day, both happy and sad. It was fun to see all my cousins that I hadn't seen in years, but sad knowing that we would be saying goodbye to Aunt Myra.

Sunday was my family reunion of the Galloway side of my family. My parents drove me to Aunt Shirley's and came inside to meet everyone with me. In addition to Aunt Shirley and Uncle Roy, I met Uncle Bob and his daughter, Cathy, and 5 siblings—Jeff, Tim, Terry, Steve, and Linda. I found out I had another brother, Barry, who was unable to attend the reunion. Steve and Linda had been born after I had been adopted. I was warmly welcomed into the family. It was so fun to meet everyone and learn about my family, my history, my background. After this, I made a couple more trips to Seattle and spent time with my birth family. We got to know each other and it was wonderful.

But my reunion story doesn't end with our reunion in 1994. In December 2005 I got a Christmas card from Uncle Bob and his daughter Cathy, and in the card was an index card with a name on it, Christina Jones. I had no idea who this was, so I wrote to Cathy and asked her. Her response? Christina is your sister. Being Christmas, I wrote to Christina and sent the letter in a Christmas card. I heard from Christina, or Tina, a short time later. She had not known about me until she had received my card and letter. Tina and I communicated often by email, and in July 2006, I flew out to Chesapeake, Virginia to meet her and her family, which included her husband and four children. I spent only a week there, and it wasn't long enough. But during that week, we learned so much about each other.

A few years after our first meeting, Tina planned to come to visit me in Minnesota. When trying to decide the best time to come, I told her the things that my city had going on every summer. The Judy Garland Festival, Showboat, Tall Timber Days, and the Fair. As soon as I mentioned the fair, she said "I love the fair!" I couldn't help but laugh. We were definitely related, as the fair was also my favorite part of summer.

Because of social media, I have reconnected with the siblings I met years ago, and we all agree that we need to keep in touch. Thinking back to my search and reunion, I am thankful that I followed my heart and found my family. But it wouldn't have happened without God to guide me. God had given me two families, and I am forever thankful and blessed.

7

THE GOLD CROSS

It has always amazed me how God uses a bad situation to teach us things. These lessons help us through things that happen, both good and bad.

In March 2009, I was blindsided by cancer. Cancer is a very scary word and the minute I heard from the oncologist, I heard nothing else. I was diagnosed with stage two uterine cancer, and surgery was scheduled for the following week at St. Mary's in Duluth, 80 miles from my home. I don't remember much about the week between diagnosis and surgery, except that I was still somewhat in shock, with all kinds of "what if" questions running through my mind.

On my first evening in the hospital, I was alone in my room, thinking about my upcoming surgery. I glanced out my window, and my eyes came to rest on a beautiful gold cross on the top of a nearby church. I remember thinking how pretty it was, but I didn't realize until later what the significance of that cross would be.

The surgery went well the next day. My time in the recovery room took a little longer as they had a hard time regulating my blood sugar and blood pressure. One was too high, the other too low. But soon they got them both under control, a huge relief.

There were times during my hospital stay when I felt discouraged, depressed, and afraid of what would happen. Fear of the unknown. By this time, I had already been told that I would need five weeks of radiation treatment. Even though the surgery had been a success, the radiation was a precautionary measure just to make sure that all was well.

During the day, I would have several family members and friends visiting me, which made the days brighter. It helped me not to think as much about my cancer or my upcoming treatments. We laughed and joked, and it was nice to have those distractions. But my evenings alone were different. I had way too much time to think about things, and I just couldn't turn my mind off. I was afraid. Afraid of the treatments. Afraid of cancer itself. Afraid they hadn't gotten it all, afraid it would someday come back. At times it was overwhelming. During one of these restless evenings, my eyes came to rest upon the gold cross outside my window. As I gazed at the cross, the words to an old hymn came into my mind…

> "Turn your eyes upon Jesus,
> look full in his wonderful face,
> and the things of earth will grow strangely dim,
> in the light of his glory and grace."

I know these words just didn't pop into my mind. The Lord put them there. He gave me those words to remind me that I needed to turn my eyes to Him, that I needed to focus on Him, that I needed to give my worries to Him, and that He would see me through.

That night changed how I looked at my situation. As a Christian, when faced with a difficult time or circumstance, turning our eyes to Jesus should be the first thing we think to do. Instead, it is often the last thing we think of because of the emotional state we might be in during the trial we are facing. And that is what happened to me when faced with this cancer diagnosis. I was so worried about my treatment and what I might be facing, that I didn't think about anything else. That is, until the gold cross. I realized that the Lord had put me in that hospital bed by that window for a reason. For the remainder of my hospital stay, and in the weeks that followed during my treatments, I remembered to keep my eyes upon Jesus. He brought me through the situation, and I have been cancer-free for fourteen years.

There's not a day that goes by that I don't think of that gold cross. It is a constant reminder to me to turn my eyes towards heaven and pray, to give thanks for the many blessings the Lord has given me, and even to thank Him for the trials and tribulations. He gives us these things to teach us to depend on Him, to trust Him, and to have faith.

On a recent trip to Duluth for my yearly cancer check, we drove past the church with the gold cross, and I was again reminded of its beauty and of its significance. I believe that God gave me that cross to bring me comfort during a very scary time in my life, and He used it to remind me of where my help and hope come from. That beautiful gold cross is forever etched in my mind and my heart.

And I praise God for the visuals He provided to uplift and sustain me. He knew just what I needed.

8

RELAY FOR LIFE

This story is dedicated to Patty Pierce, our good friend, co-worker, and RFL team member who lost her battle with cancer. Patty was a wonderful person who was an inspiration to us and is greatly missed by all who were blessed to have known her.

❀

*J*t is often true that good things do come out of a bad situation. A bad situation can bring about unexpected blessings. That was the case in 2009 after I was diagnosed with cancer, and I had surgery along with five weeks of radiation treatment.

My good friend Sue suggested that now we

should get involved with Relay for Life. I had never heard of this before, so she explained that it was a big fundraiser for the American Cancer Society. My first experience with Relay was in the summer of 2009 when Sue and I went to see what it was all about. It was like nothing we had ever experienced before. There was live entertainment on the stage, and they read a list of cancer survivors that were there. The survivors did the survivor walk around the park. There was food, and the park was surrounded by luminaries that had been purchased and decorated in memory of someone who had lost their battle with cancer or in honor of someone who had survived this horrible disease. After spending the evening at this event, Sue and I knew that we needed to be involved. We needed to do our part to help raise money for this wonderful cause, Cancer had touched our lives, as well as the lives of many friends and family members.

By the following summer, Sue and I had encouraged friends, family, and co-workers to join our Relay for Life team, and together we named our team The La De Da Divas. As Sue and I were the captain and co-captain of our team, we attended the monthly Relay for Life meetings. We met the most wonderful people who made us feel right at home and part of the group. Relay for Life was an overnight event. Each team would set up a campsite that fit the theme.

One year we had an ugly hat contest where each team decorated a hat. They had a trophy for the best campsite. Each year, the team that won the trophy had to add something that would represent their team. Our team won once and we were proud of our accomplishments.

One year as we walked around the park reading the luminaries, we counted them. There were well over 1000 luminaries lighting up the sidewalks.

As our team became more involved in the RFL, we would have our own fundraising events during the year, before the RFL event in July. We would have Christmas bake sales, and in the spring we would have a large rummage sale. We also had pancake breakfasts at Applebees and sold luminaries that we would decorate and put along the sidewalk on the night of RFL. During our first year as an RFL team, we won the bronze award for the $500 we had raised. During our fifth year, we won a gold award for the large amount of money we had raised.

It was during our fifth year that we decided as a team to step down. It had been a good five-year run, but we all knew it was time. Many of our team members were going through life-changing events and needed to focus on those rather than RFL. It has been eight years since The La De Da Divas stepped down.

We no longer have an RFL event located in our area, which is sad because it was such a fun time and a worthy cause. I often reflect on the five years we were involved in this event, and I have such wonderful memories. But the most treasured memories are the friends I made, and how God turned my bad situation into a time of blessings, blessings that will forever be in my heart.

9

THROUGH THE EYES OF A CHILD

On February 21, 2022, President's Day, I read a story on Facebook that I immediately knew I wanted to include in my book.

The story was written by Naomi Bickel, the daughter of a dear friend. I contacted Naomi and she graciously permitted me to share her story.

My prayer is that you, my readers, will find this story to be an inspiration, as I did.

On Presidents Day 30 years ago, my family's house burned down. We lost absolutely everything. But that day was an answer to a prayer I'd been praying for months.

Let me rewind and explain. At some point during the summer of 1991, I found myself lying in bed trying to fall asleep, when suddenly something in the dark caught my eye. In the space between my bedroom door and the floor, I saw a single flame. It was small but vibrant and as I watched it dance I just knew our house was going to burn down. Not in that moment, but eventually. I immediately began to pray and beg God not to let our house burn down. I saw that flame many times over the following months and it always reminded me to pray. I prayed out loud, silently. I even wrote out prayers in my trapper keeper binder.

After several months, I realized something. I was praying for the wrong thing! I was as sure of that as I was that my house was going to burn down. So, I changed my prayer to something that felt right. I began to ask God to protect my family and to keep safe the firefighters that would eventually respond to that call.

Months later while visiting family about 45 minutes from our house, the phone rang. It was our neighbor from across the highway. Our house was on fire and she'd been calling our whole family trying to find out if anyone knew where we were. She was panicked. You see, it was President's Day so there was no school. We should have all been home. As we pulled into our long driveway, the firetrucks were slowly turning onto the highway. I was relieved because there were no ambulances no screaming sirens, they were in no hurry to leave, so clearly no one was injured. My family was safe, all the fire-fighters were safe. And God was good!

Some may question that last statement considering our house still burned down and we still lost absolutely everything we owned. But that single flame was a seed undefeated. Before the Fire Marshall even left our yard that afternoon, both the Salvation Army and the Red Cross were there, with checks and vouchers to JCPenney. That JCPenney detail isn't arbitrary either. You see, we didn't have much money, so most of our clothing and toys were second-hand. There's nothing wrong with that, but in my 7-year-old eyes, that meant only rich people shopped at the mall! Only rich people could afford to buy new clothes from an expensive store.

The next day my brother and I couldn't go to school until after we bought something to wear. We waited for the mall to open, bought and donned our new outfits, and arrived at school just after lunch.

The moment we walked into our small Christian school we were greeted by an entryway filled with boxes and bags piled halfway to the ceiling. I had no idea what was happening. I thought there had been some charity drive that I'd forgotten and felt bad that I didn't show up with whatever it was I was supposed to bring! In class that day I found out that everything in that entryway was for us. Somehow, someone had contacted all the radio stations and churches and told everyone in town that a single mom with two kids had just lost everything to a house fire. Someone coordinated the whole thing without our knowledge, opened the school, and managed all the donations. Thanks to God and all His faithful servants, less than 24 hours after our house and everything in it burned to the ground, we had more clothes, books, and toys than we'd ever had before.

So, to anyone out there who is struggling, facing disaster, or wondering if God even cares, He does. Whatever storm you're facing, there's a purpose and a plan for you. He is faithful. Let Jesus be the flame in those dark hours.

Our Lord alone can give beauty for ashes, turn mourning into joy, and despair into praise (Isaiah 61:13).

We lost our house, but He protected what was

important, and buried our loss beneath a massive pile of unexpected blessings.

Thank you to anyone and everyone who helped my family during that time. To this day, I have no idea who did all that work behind the scenes, but I am very grateful.

Thanks for reading and God bless you!

10

GOD IS ABLE

"I'm very blessed that my friend and fellow writer Rena Yeager wanted to use my stories in her book. She not only has my permission, but my blessing. I hope you as the reader will know that looking back on everything I've been through in my life, I was never alone. Thank you and God bless you." Karen Grife

Ephesians 3:20-21 Now to him who is able to do far more abundantly than all that we ask or think, according to the power at work within us, to him be glory in the church and in Christ Jesus throughout all generations, forever and ever.

*W*hen I was a child, phonics and spelling were drilled into our heads. The teachers thought memorization was the only way children learned, and for most, this worked very well. But for a few of us, it didn't. Learning disabilities are real and affect more children than they realize.

I would like people to know that they don't have to be ashamed or embarrassed because they have difficulties with reading, spelling, or any other subject. Nowadays, they would say attention deficit disorder, dyslexia, autism, or a myriad of other diagnoses they find in children today. But when I was a child 60 years ago, the teachers called us unruly, willful, disobedient, or stupid. And that in itself came with a mindset and a life full of shame.

I grew up with three older sisters and one younger. Five girls from August 1950 to January 1956. I felt lost in a crowd even in my own family. I had great parents, and they worked very hard to make sure we had everything we needed for a happy and healthy life.

I always had trouble sitting still in school, which was required for many hours a day. My mind wandered. I found it hard to concentrate on anything that had to do with school. In the second grade, I was miserable. Unless you can pay attention, you miss much of what the teacher is saying. There were times we were supposed to read quietly by ourselves, and that was a total waste of time because I would be thinking of anything but reading.

My experience with other classmates was never good. My inability to read in front of them was horrifying for me, and oral spelling bees made me physically ill. The other students found it very humorous that I couldn't read, or even sound out some of the simple words. Back then there wasn't much extra help in the classrooms for the students that were behind, and teachers didn't have time to spend their days helping those kids. Some teachers were very sympathetic, and others weren't.

As I went into third grade, I had a new teacher. She was not a patient teacher. She also had her favorite students, and I wasn't one of them. With teachers like this, she felt if you didn't work up to her expectations you were willful, stupid, or lazy, and she took every opportunity to insinuate as much. I now believe that I could have had ADHD, as well as other undiagnosed learning disabilities. She didn't have time for students that she felt didn't try, as she told me that many times. Instead of allowing me to sit in the back so I didn't distract the other students with my fidgeting, she felt I needed to sit up front so she could keep an eye on me. She felt that was the way to get me over being willful. It didn't work. I was held back that year, which also added to my insecurities. The stigma of being different and the shame of being held back I felt for the rest of my school years.

One of my earliest recollections of failure was during an oral spelling bee. The teacher gave me words she knew I could spell. The other students laughed because they knew the words were too simple. After a while, she gave me a word I didn't know just to make it fair for the students who could spell. The teacher was trying to give me more confidence and help me overcome my anxiety, which in the long run made me feel even worse because all I wanted to do was sit down and not have to try anymore. I never remember winning a spelling bee or acing any other test in school.

After a while, I learned to be invisible, or so I thought. Soon I wouldn't be called on to answer questions in class. I worked just hard enough to get passing grades. I probably would have cheated, but never figured out how to do that without getting caught.

I hated school. It was the worst experience of my life. Every subject had its challenges. Even math, which was my best subject. But I couldn't do the word problems. I couldn't figure out what exactly they wanted because I couldn't read.

As time went on, I kept very much to myself. I was still teased by others and hated the fact that I felt too stupid already. After all, my dad couldn't read, and he was a great man. I found it easier to get lost in junior high and just get by without anyone knowing my shame or problems. If I got my work done on time, the teachers wouldn't be concerned about how well I did. My grades reflected my inability, but the teachers just thought I was slower than the average students. I kept to myself and stayed out of trouble.

The spring I was fifteen I met a man. He was twenty-one. He had just gotten out of the Navy. He was a good-looking man, with big dimples on each cheek and dark curly hair. He was also the biggest sweet-talker I had ever known, By the middle of summer, we were in love. So, when he asked me to marry him, I said yes. It was not only a start to the life I longed for, which included a home of my own and children, but it was also a way to get out of the place I hated. Looking back, I think not having to go to school was more appealing than being married. I turned sixteen in August. I was able to drop out of school in October, and we were married in November, very much against my parents' wishes.

I thought this was the end of my reading problems. No more being teased for what I couldn't do. I would start my new life, and no one knew my secret. I thought I could read well enough and even though my spelling was terrible I thought I would get by.

Our marriage was good for a while. In 1975, I got my GED so I officially had my diploma, which I was very proud of. We had three beautiful children to show for the years we were together.

When my kids started school, I was excited and yet had apprehensions at the same time. It wasn't long before they were asking me how to spell a word. Sometimes I would have to tell them I didn't know, and they would have to ask their dad. I was not expecting the one person I loved would make jokes about the fact that I couldn't spell. So here it was again, the same feelings of inadequacy. I dealt with it differently this time. I didn't run and hide. I couldn't These were my kids, so I bought a good dictionary and taught them how to use it. We all learned the process of using it. I grew more confident as I taught my children. I never realized I couldn't let what people said about me influence my life forever. After many years, I came to the realization I could no longer let my learning disabilities affect my life. No one is perfect, we all have struggles, and everyone makes mistakes.

When I got a divorce in 1982, my parents helped move the kids and me back to my hometown. It was about this same time that I came to know the Lord Jesus Christ. A lot happened that year that changed my life. Jesus changed my life. I learned that he loved me just as I was. His unconditional love changed me. My ability to read and spell began to improve as I read the bible and followed the Lord.

By 1984 I was remarried to a sweet and wonderful man. I had my fourth child. Life was good. I started writing poetry, but I felt there was so much more to say. My husband was a great encouragement and even became my proofreader.

When I was fifty and all the children were grown and on their own, I went to college. I know the Lord gave me the desire to write for children. I needed to brush up on English. I started writing poetry but then focused on children's books. I was so blessed by the Lord through college. I graduated with high honors. I have written many children's books, and now the Lord has given me many ideas to write for older readers. I will continue to write as long as I am able.

My journey was not always easy. There were painful experiences. But I wouldn't be who I am today without those experiences. I have so much empathy for anyone with a disability or who may be a little different. I am thankful for my journey and truly believe it was all a God thing.

11

NOT THE LIFE WE PLANNED

"Another story of my life, and the never-ending love of God. Even in my pain and the loss of my husband, I never lost my faith and love for my Savior Jesus Christ."
Karen Grife

When a couple meets, falls in love, and gets married, their expectations for the future are great. They never imagine their lives being turned upside down, especially in just three short years.

I became a Christian about the same time I met my second husband, Luke. These two events changed my life forever. Luke and I were married in July 1983. At age twenty-six, Luke took on the responsibility of a ready-made family, which included my three children. We also decided to have another child. On August 17, 1984, Josiah Eric was born. We lived a very full and active life with Luke working at Potlatch in Grand Rapids, while I stayed home and took care of the kids.

Over the next several years, we went through some very difficult times. We lost everything in a house fire. My older kids' dad passed away a week later. And I became very sick for about six months. But through it all, I knew the Lord was with us. Luke and I remained close, still very much in love. We lived in town for a few years, but trying to keep track of four kids in town was not an easy task. We made plans to get property out of town and build our own home. With a lot of help from our parents, we were in our garage home in just a few months.

Then things began to change. I had recovered from the fungus disease I had contracted from my cat. Luke had been sick with what we thought was a flu that seemed to last a long time. When he got over it, he started experiencing severe pain throughout his whole body. We thought it was just part of the flu that just hadn't left. This lasted a couple of weeks before he finally went to the doctor. After a year of continuing to get worse and doctors not knowing what was causing the pain. Luke was sent to a rheumatologist. There was test after test. They determined that Luke had five kinds of arthritis, along with back problems that required surgery. The Orthopedic specialist said he "would fix him right up." So, in good faith, Luke had surgery. But in fact, the surgery did not help Luke's pain.

From the time he woke up in the hospital his right foot was numb, and his back pain was still there. The specialist admitted that Luke's back was in much worse shape than he had suspected, and during surgery, they had severed a nerve in his foot. It wasn't too long after the surgery that Luke lost his job because he was no longer able to do the basic duties that the job required, like going up and down stairs, standing for more than twenty minutes at a time, or being able to lift over ten pounds. These were the limitations the doctor put on him. And along with not being able to do the things that he used to, came feelings of worthlessness, depression, and shame. He felt he could no longer provide for his family.

Luke was a very private person and didn't show his feelings to anyone but me. He didn't want people to feel sorry for him. He hid his problems and because of this, people thought he was doing much better than he truly was. They didn't see the days when he could hardly move, his lack of enthusiasm for anything in life, or the pain I saw on his face.

People also believe the only one affected by his disability was Luke. But they were wrong! From the smallest problem to the overall picture, the whole family was affected. Especially our son, Josiah. Many things his dad should have been a part of were now left to me.

There was a time when we bought property and had planned to build a house. We got the garage built and made that livable until we could get the house built. But when Luke lost his job, our income went to almost nothing and the house never happened. Instead of looking forward to a long, stable, and healthy life together, we filled our lives with doctor appointments and trips to the Duluth clinic. We just tried to live day by day. Without the peace, Joy, and strength from the Lord, I know I wouldn't have made it.

It took four years of trying, but eventually Luke got on social security disability. That helped ease our minds and the financial burden we were experiencing. As time went on, Luke's personality started to change. Due to arthritis in his neck, he started having headaches every day. The doctors had him on massive painkillers. He became even more withdrawn and much quieter. He was an avid reader but soon that was also a thing of the past. He lost interest in doing much of anything. No more hunting, fishing, long walks, star gazing, or even talking for hours on end. It was all lost. Luke tried to help and join in, but soon he would just head back to the house. I felt so bad for him because I knew how much he was hurting, and all the pain medications he was on. All I could do was pray for him.

I handled everything that came along with as much strength and support as I could muster, but the one who lost the most other than Luke was Josiah. He was eight years old at the time Luke started changing, and even though Luke was still a good father, he couldn't do everything a son needs from a dad. Our other kids were grown by this time and doing their own thing. Josiah essentially lost out on everything that most other young men have their dads for. I did the best I could to help Josiah with what he needed me to do.

Even though Luke was not the man I had married twenty years earlier, he was still a kind and gentle man, soft-spoken and grateful for everything I did for him. Through the pain and all the drugs and the disappointments in our lives, I still loved him. He was my best friend. Through all of my prayers and with the help from the church we were attending, Luke also committed to the Lord. What an answer to prayer! We prayed for Luke's healing, but no one is guaranteed a perfect future. All we could do was carry on. I know I would not have made it without the Lord.

In 2010, we discovered Luke had Renal Cell Carcinoma, and we kept praying. The doctors immediately scheduled surgery. They operated on March eighth. The supposed two-hour surgery took five hours. When the doctor came in after they were done with surgery, he was hopeful that they had gotten all the cancer, but he couldn't be sure.

We prayed and believed that Luke would be healed and that the Lord would do it in His own way. On May twelfth, 2010, at age 56, Luke went home to be with the Lord. No more pain, no more drugs, no more doctors, and no more living with disabilities. And that is a God thing!

It was the hardest day of my life. To lose the man I thought I would spend the rest of my life with. Twenty-six years of marriage ended, and twenty-six years of taking care of each other were all gone. The next few days were filled with making plans for his celebration of life. I started helping the family through all the emotions of losing someone very special in their lives, especially Josiah. I was never good at making decisions on my own. I guess now was the time to start. If I hadn't had a relationship with the Lord, I never would have made it through such a time as this. The Lord gave the peace, comfort, strength, and belief to know that Luke was not hurting anymore and that he was in Heaven.

My life goes on, even though I don't know what that looks like. I do know Jesus is my rock and my provider, the source of my strength and peace. Forever.

ACKNOWLEDGMENTS

I would like to thank the following people…

To my beta readers Kim, Karen, and Sue, who read my stories, corrected errors, and made suggestions to improve them.

To Kim Wood, my dear friend, encourager, and supporter, who inspired this book's writing during one of our daily conversations.

To Karen Grife, my dear friend, also a writer, who encouraged me to keep writing and shared her stories in this book.

To Sue Jones, my close friend of over 20 years, who always supports me and stands by me.

To my friend Linda Bauer, a close friend for over 50 years, 50+ years blessed!

To Bev Landey, a good friend who encourages me and supports me.

To Ralna English, an inspiration to many through her music and kindness. A favorite singer in my teenage years, and a treasured friend in my adulthood.

To Toni Brose and her crew at Bubbles and Bows who supported me and took such good care of Lexi always, especially during the past year when her health was declining. Toni is not just my groomer; she is my friend.

To Tom and Judi Stecker, the wonderful family who took Radar into their home loved him, and gave him a home when I could no longer do so.

To Jeani Bumgarner, if it hadn't been for her, we would not have found our precious puppies.

To Naomi Bickel, who graciously allowed me to use her story in this book.

To my good friend Gina Hill, who invited me to do book signings at her table during craft shows, and who took care of Lexi from puppyhood till the end.

ABOUT THE AUTHOR

 Rena Yeager was born in Everett Washington and raised in Northern Minnesota. She discovered her passion for writing at the age of 14.

After graduating from college, Rena worked in the field of childcare, including co-owning a daycare center with a friend for three years. She also worked in children's ministries at her church for over 20 years.

In 1995, Rena made a career change, and for the past thirty years has devoted her life to working with people with disabilities, both in their home setting and in the Special Olympics.

Rena lives in Northern Minnesota with her Shitese (Shih Tzu/Maltese), Gracie Ruth.

Read Rena's blog at: https://www.alaskadp.com

 pinterest.com/ryeager1961
instagram.com/ryeager1961

Also by Alaska Dreams Publishing

Please visit www.alaskadp.com to see these titles:

Also by Rena Yeager:

Inspiring Special Needs Stories (https://amzn.to/3II0AON)

By William Casselman:

Alaska Freedom Brigade | Rookie | Apache Snow | In Search of Honor | The Six Book Revelation Series | Legend of Silene | Blake's War

The Alaska Off-Grid Survival Series by Miles Martin:

Going Wild | Gone Wild | Still Wild | Beyond Wild | Back To Wild | Surviving Wild | Secretly Wild | Retiring Wild

Titles by other ADP authors:

My Life In The Wilderness | All Over The Road | Ghost Cave Mountain | Inside the Circle | The Silver Horn of Robin Hood | Alaskan Troll Eggs | Through My Eyes | The Professional Ghost Investigator | The Adventures of Jason and Bo | Seeds Of The Pirate Rebels